GOD OF
miracles

GORDON MOORE

Ark House Press
PO Box 1722, Port Orchard, WA 98366 USA
PO Box 1321, Mona Vale NSW 1660 Australia
PO Box 318 334, West Harbour, Auckland 0661 New Zealand
arkhousepress.com

© 2020 Gordon J. Moore

All Scriptures are quoted from the New King James Version (NKJV) unless otherwise stated.

All rights reserved. No part of this publication may be reproduced, stored in a retrieval system or transmitted in any form or by any means electronic, mechanical, photocopying, recording or otherwise without the prior written permission of the publisher.

Cataloguing in Publication Data:
Title: God of Miracles
ISBN: 978-0-6489380-0-2 (pbk.)
Subjects: Leadership
Other Authors/Contributors: Moore, Gordon J

Published with Gordon J Moore
PO Box 46 Aspley Qld 4034 AUSTRALIA

COVER PICTURE: M51 Cross of Hubble

The cover picture is of the core of the nearby spiral galaxy M51, taken with the Wide Planetary camera on NASA's Hubble Space Telescope. The size of the image is 1100 light years! Here we see the miraculous, redemptive cross signature of God displayed in the universes.
Our God is 'THE GOD OF MIRACLES'!

*"Yet He Himself bore our SICKNESSES,
and He carried our PAINS:
but we in turn regarded Him stricken,
struck down by God, and afflicted.
But He was pierced because of our transgressions,
crushed because of our iniquities:
punishment for our peace was on Him;
and we are HEALED by His wounds."
Isaiah 53:4-5 HCSB*

CONTENTS

Dedication		ix
Acknowledgements		xi
Introduction		xiii
Chapter One	Miracles Can Happen!	1
Chapter Two	Divine Healing In The Atonement	5
Chapter Three	Divine Healing Through The Scriptures	23
Chapter Four	Why Christ Heals	40
Chapter Five	Divine Healing In Your Faith	53
Chapter Six	Healing And The Ministry Of Laying On Of Hands	68
Chapter Seven	Believing In The Wait	73
Conclusion	God's Priority Is The Healing Of Your Soul	87
Bibliography		97

DEDICATION

This book is dedicated to all who are sick and in pain in their bodies.

It is written to declare to you the Good News that our Lord Jesus Christ provided healing and wholeness for you through His perfect, atoning work on the Cross.

> *"Who His own self bare our sins in*
> *His own body on the tree,*
> *that we, being dead to sins, should*
> *live unto righteousness;*
> *by Whose stripes you were healed."*
> *1Peter 2:24*

ACKNOWLEDGEMENTS

The contents of this book are the story of a personal journey of faith and experience.

It is the result of a combination of influences. What I saw. What I was taught. What I read and my personal revelation and experience.

In particular, I owe so much to my home church senior pastor, Ken Wright. He modelled, taught and personally showed me how to minister divine healing to people through the exercise of faith, the Word of Knowledge and impartation through the laying on of hands.

As a result of this rich background and heritage, I began my own personal journey of discovery. This led me to the writings and ministries of divine healing pioneers such as F.F. Bosworth, John G. Lake, Gordon Lindsay, Oral Roberts, T.L. Osborne and Harry Greenwood and others.

I acknowledge all of these heroes of faith and their invaluable insights and revelations in the healing power of God.

To a New Level

In the early 1980's I was invited by Stuart Gramenz, director of "Jesus Heals India" to be part of his preaching team throughout east and northern India.

I will never forget one evening in one of those 'Jesus Heals' meetings. A desperate Hindu mother came carrying her child in her arms who was born crippled for healing.

I laid my hands on the child's head. With tears in my eyes I believed for a miracle. I instructed the mother, who was standing on the other side of the platform to call her child. When she called, the child stood to her feet and ran to her mother totally healed!

The place went ballistic at the sight of this miracle and that night many miracles were released. I was overcome with joy and amazement at what God just did. I was changed forever. *Our God is the God of Miracles!*

INTRODUCTION

Everywhere I travel, I meet so many people who are suffering with sickness and pain. People who are unaware that the Lord Jesus Christ has made provision for them. Provision both for their salvation spiritually and for their physical healing and health through His work on the cross of Calvary.

> *"Yet He Himself bore our sicknesses,*
> *and He carried our pains:*
> *but we in turn regarded Him stricken,*
> *struck down by God, and afflicted.*
> *But He was pierced because of our transgressions,*
> *crushed because of our iniquities:*
> *punishment for our peace was on Him;*
> *and we are healed by His wounds."*
> *Isaiah 53:4-5 (HCSB)*

I have rewritten this book, previously entitled "*With Healing in His Wings*" (1984), in order to update and recommit to writing some of the material that I have shared over many years on the subject of divine healing.

This is not an attempt to present an exhaustive theological treatise on the subject, nor is it to prove, or defend the truths of divine healing. Rather it is to provide a declaration of Christ's atoning, healing power which has been made available to all who will believe and receive.

Once we are convinced in our minds and hearts that divine healing is God's provision in Christ for us, we will be able to boldly ask in faith for a miracle of healing from the Lord Jesus Christ.

The words of Gordon Lindsey ably express this conviction:-

"The question no longer is, 'Does God heal today?'

Rather, to the individual in need of healing it is, 'since so many are being healed, what must I do to be delivered also?'"

It is my sincere prayer that as you read this book, you also will be encouraged and strengthened in your faith to reach out to our Lord Jesus Christ and discover your healing and health.

Gordon Moore
AUTHOR

CHAPTER ONE

MIRACLES CAN HAPPEN!

*"But Jesus beheld them, and said to them,
With men this is impossible;
but with God all things are possible."
Matt 19:26*

The starting point for all miracles is found in God Himself, Who by His very nature is a supernatural, miracle working God. Well, not to Him, because God is just 'naturally super'!

In fact, to deny that miracles can happen, is to deny the very existence, nature and power of God.

All the works of God from the very beginning of creation are supernatural, miraculous, marvellous and beyond human thinking, comprehension and ability.

*"Many, Lord, my God, are the wonderful
works which You have done,
and Your thoughts which are toward us.
They can't be declared back to You.
If I would declare and speak of them, they
are more than can be numbered."
Ps 40:5 WEB Translation*

Isaiah, the prophet began to consider the miraculous works of God and came to the conclusion that we are all like a "drop in a bucket" compared to God.

*"Who has measured the waters
in the hollow of His hand,
and meted out heaven with the span,
and comprehended the dust of
the earth in a measure,
and weighed the mountains in scales,
and the hills in a balance?
Who has directed the Spirit of the Lord, or
being His counsellor has taught Him?
With whom took He counsel,
and who instructed Him,
and taught Him in the path of judgment,
and taught Him knowledge,*

*and showed to Him the way of understanding?
Behold, the nations are as a drop of a bucket,
and are counted as the small dust of the balance:
behold, He takes up the isles as a very little thing."*
Is 45:12-14

Even looking within ourselves, like King David, we can only marvel at the creative genius, power and wonder of God in creating us.

*"I will praise You; for I am fearfully and
wonderfully made: marvellous are Your
works; and that my soul knows right well.
My substance was not hid from You, when I
was made in secret, and curiously wrought
in the lowest parts of the earth.
Your eyes did see my substance,
yet being imperfect;
and in Your book all my members were written,
which in continuance were fashioned,
when as yet there was none of them.
How precious also are Your thoughts to me,
O God! How great is the sum of them!
If I should count them, they are more
in number than the sand:*

when I awake, I am still with You."
Ps 139:14-18

If God has done all of these incredible things, then, miracles of healing for today are certainly not beyond His divine ability and power...***MIRACLES CAN HAPPEN!!!***

CHAPTER TWO

DIVINE HEALING IN THE ATONEMENT

"And not only so, but we also joy in God through our Lord Jesus Christ, by Whom we have now received the atonement."
Romans 5:11

The truth of atonement is central to the Christian faith. Atonement is the redeeming action of God to cancel, cleanse, and expiate the sin and condemnation and all of its effects from mankind in order to reconcile all people to Himself.

The Lord Jesus Christ accomplished atonement for us through His redeeming work on the cross of Calvary.

> *"And He (Jesus) is the propitiation (expiation)*
> *for our sins; and not for ours only, but also*
> *from the sins of the whole world."*
> *1John 2:2*

The Old Testament is rich in pictures that foretell Christ's atoning work on the cross of Calvary.

1. The Passover Lamb – The Passover Lamb (Exodus 12:1-28), is an Old Testament picture and 'type' of Christ as our lamb sacrificed for us to take away our sins.

> *"The next day John sees Jesus*
> *coming unto him, and says,*
> *behold the Lamb of God, who takes*
> *away the sin of the world."*
> *John 1:29*

> *"Purge out therefore the old leaven, that*
> *you may be a new lump. As you are*
> *unleavened. For even Christ our*
> *Passover is sacrificed for us."*
> *1Corinthians 5:7*

It is clear from the Scriptures that Jesus Christ is our Lamb sacrificed for us. He was the one Who knew no sin, yet He was made sin for us.

> *"Forasmuch as you know that you were not redeemed with corruptible things, as silver and gold, from your vain conversation received by tradition from your fathers; but with the precious blood of Christ, as of a lamb without blemish and without spot."*
> *1Peter 1:18-19*

When God instituted the Passover Feast, there were two things that the Israelites were to do with the lamb.

First, the blood was to be applied. This was done in order to escape judgment when the angel of death passed over the nation of Egypt. When the angel of God saw the blood sprinkled on the doorpost and on the lintel of a house, he would 'pass over' and that house would escape judgment.

This speaks of the blood of Christ providing escape from the judgement of God which all of us are worthy of because of our sins.

> *"And according to the law almost all*
> *things are purified with blood,*
> *and without shedding of blood this is no remission.*
> *And as it is appointed for men to die*
> *once, but after this the judgement,*
> *so Christ was once offered once*
> *to bear the sins of many.*
> *To those who eagerly wait for Him*
> *He will appear a second time,*
> *apart from sin, for salvation."*
> *Hebrews 9:22, 27-28*

Second, the lamb's flesh was to be eaten. On that first Passover night the Children of Israel were to roast a lamb and eat it after sprinkling it's blood upon the doorposts and the lintel of their houses. They were to dress themselves and be ready for the journey ahead.

This speaks of God's provision for physical strength and health for the journey. It was God's provision for their physical bodies to be prepared for the exodus journey from the land of Egypt on the Passover evening.

The Passover lamb provided both spiritual and physical needs of God's people.

2. The Covenant at Marah

After the children of Israel had experienced the incredible delivering power of God on that Passover night and the subsequent deliverance through the waters of the Red Sea, they came to the waters of Marah. But as we read the waters were bitter and they could not drink from the waters. The children of Israel lifted up their voice and murmured. And so Moses cried to the Lord and the Lord revealed Himself in His redemptive Name Jehovah Raphah; "*I am the Lord Who heals you.*"

> *"So he cried out to the Lord, and*
> *the Lord showed him a tree;*
> *and when he cast it into the waters,*
> *the waters were made sweet.*
> *There He made a statute and*
> *an ordinance for them.*
> *And there He tested them, and said, if you*
> *diligently heed the voice of the Lord your*
> *God and do what is right in His sight,*
> *give ear to His commandments*
> *and keep all His statutes,*
> *I will put none of the diseases on you*
> *which I have brought on the Egyptians.*
> *For I am the Lord who heals you."*

Exodus 15:25-26

Here we read the amazing words *"the Lord showed Moses a tree."* Here we see the wonder of Scripture. The Lord showed Moses a tree because He was teaching his people that healing was to come by way of a tree through Christ.

*"Christ has redeemed us from the curse of the law,
being made a curse for us; for it is written,
cursed is everyone that hangs on a tree."
Galatians 3:13*

All the bitter waters of life can be made sweet through the healing work of the cross of Christ.

Very little comment needs to be made in order to interpret or explain this picture, or type of Christ. It is clear that the cross (or "tree") of Christ is portrayed in the Old Testament waters of Marah as a place of physical healing.

*"Who His own self bare our sins in
His own body on the tree,
that we, being dead to sin, should
live unto righteousness;
by Whose stripes you were healed."
1Peter 2:24*

3. The Brazen Serpent

As Israel journeyed in the wilderness the Bible reveals that they became discouraged in their journey and began to speak against God and Moses. They accused God of bringing them into the wilderness to die. They even complained about the manna that God had wonderfully provided for food.

So the Lord judged their sin of complaining by sending fiery serpents among them which had bitten the people and many died. Realising their sin, the people came to Moses repenting and asking him to pray to the Lord so that He would remove the serpents.

> *So Moses prayed to the Lord, and the Lord instructed Moses to "make a bronze serpent and set it on a pole; and it shall be that everyone who is bitten when he looks at it shall live." (Numbers 21:8)*

In obedience to the Lord's command Moses made a bronze serpent and placed it on a pole and instructed the people that whoever looked at this serpent on the pole would live. And the Bible records that *"everyone who looked, lived."* (Numbers 21:9)

The bronze serpent lifted up in the wilderness provided two things for the children of Israel who looked upon it.

First, they were forgiven of their sin against the Lord and judgement was lifted from them.

Second, they were healed from the poison from the snake bite which was bringing death to their physical bodies.

So we see that the serpent on the pole in the wilderness provided forgiveness for sin, and healing for bodies.

In John's gospel Jesus spoke this of Himself foretelling of His crucifixion on the cross:-

> *"And as Moses lifted up the*
> *serpent in the wilderness,*
> *even so must the Son of Man be lifted up,*
> *that whoever believes in Him,*
> *should not perish but have eternal life."*
> *John 3:14-15*

Our Lord Jesus Christ declared here that He was fulfilling the picture and type of Scripture in that just as the serpent was lifted up for the forgiveness of sin, and the healing of the body, so He would be lifted up on the Cross to forgive men of their sins and heal them of their sicknesses.

4. The Seven Redemptive Names of God

God progressively revealed Himself through the Scriptures to man by revealing His names that describe His person.

Finally, He climaxed that revelation of Himself in the person of the Lord Jesus Christ.

"God, who at various times and in different ways spoke in time past to the fathers by the prophets, has in these last days spoken to us by His Son."
Hebrews 1:1-2

"For in Him (Jesus Christ) dwells all the fullness of the Godhead bodily. And you are complete in Him..."
Col 2:9-10

These seven, compound, redemptive names of God, find their ultimate fulfilment and embodiment in the Redeemer Himself, the Lord Jesus Christ.

The following are the seven redemptive names of God:-

(a) **"JEHOVAH SHAMMAH"** - "The Lord is there, or ever present" (Ezekiel 48:35)

Our Lord Jesus fulfilled this in His promise, *"Lo, I am with you always, even unto the end of the age"* (Matthew 28:20), and, *"For where two or three are gathered together in My Name, I am there in the midst of them."* (Matthew 18:20).

(b) **"JEHOVAH NISSI"** – "The Lord is our banner, victor, captain" (Genesis 22:14)

Our Lord Jesus Christ is our victor and captain, the banner of our salvation. *"Thanks be to God, Who gives us the victory through our Lord Jesus Christ"* (1Corinthians 15:57), and, *"Having disarmed principalities and powers, He made a public spectacle of them triumphing over them in it (the Cross)."* (Colossians 2:15)

(c) **"JEHOVAH- JIRAH"** – "The Lord our provider" (Genesis 22:14)

Our Lord Jesus Christ is the source of our provision. *"He who did not spare His own Son, but delivered Him up for us all, how shall He not with Him also freely give us all things?"* (Romans 8:32), and, *"My God shall supply all your need according to His riches in glory by Christ Jesus."* (Philippians 4:19)

(d) **"JEHOVAH RA-AH"** – "The Lord is my shepherd" (Psalm 23:1)

Our Lord Jesus Christ as the one who gave His life for His sheep has become that great Shepherd and Bishop of our souls. *"I am the Good Shepherd. The Good Shepherd gives His life for the sheep"* (John 10:11), and, *"Now may the God of peace who brought up our Lord Jesus from the dead, that great Shepherd of the sheep, through the blood of the everlasting covenant."* (Hebrews 13:20)

(e) **"JEHOVAH SHALOM"** – "The Lord is our peace" (Judges 6:24)

Through the atoning work on the Cross our Lord Jesus Christ has become our peace.

"For He Himself is our peace Who has made both one, and has broken down the middle wall of separation" (Ephesians 2:14), and, *"Therefore having been justified*

by faith, we have peace with God through our Lord Jesus Christ." (Romans 5:1)

(f) **"JEHOVAH ZIDKENU"** – "The Lord our righteousness" (Jeremiah 23:6)

The Lord Jesus Christ has given us the gift of righteousness through the grace of God. *"For if by one man's offence death reigned through one, much more those who receive abundance of grace and of the gift or righteousness will reign in life through the One, Jesus Christ"* (Romans 5:17), and, *"For He made Him who knew no sin to be sin for us, that we might become the righteousness of God in Him."* (2Corinthians 5:21)

(g) **"JEHOVAH RAPHA"** – "I am the Lord who heals you" (Exodus 15 v 26)

The Lord Jesus Christ fulfilled this redemptive name of God by healing all who came to Him. *"When evening had come, they brought to Him many who were demon-possessed. And He cast out the spirits with a word, and He healed all who were sick, that it might be fulfilled which was spoken by Isaiah the prophet, saying: He Himself took our infirmities and bore our sicknesses."* (Matthew 8:16-17)

Just as surely as our Lord Jesus Christ is our ever present Lord, our victor, our provider, our shepherd, our peace, our righteousness, HE IS OUR LORD WHO HEALS US!

5. The Prophecy of Isaiah Chapter 53

This chapter in the book of Isaiah is generally accepted as the great redemption chapter foretelling the work of Christ on the cross of Calvary.

A key to unlocking the true significance of this prophecy is to study the Hebrew words.

The two Hebrew words "choli" ("sickness") and "makob" ("pains") have been commonly translated into "griefs and sorrows" in English. Dr. Young's translation is very helpful in clarifying these words and their significance:-

> *"He is despised and left of men,*
> *a man of **pains** (makob) and*
> *acquainted with **sickness** (choli).*

*Surely our **sickness** (choli) He hath borne,*
*and our **pains** (makob) He hath carried them,*
and we – we have esteemed Him plagued,
smitten of God and afflicted.
And He is pierced for our transgressions,
bruised for our iniquities,
the chastisement of our peace was upon Him,
and by His bruise there is healing to us.
And Jehovah was delighted to bruise Him,
He has made Him sick (choli)."
Isaiah 53:3-5,10 (Youngs Literal Translation)

The Hebrew English Bible by Dr. Isaac Leeser confirms the accuracy of this translation:-

"He is despised and shunned of men;
*a man of **pains** and acquainted with **disease**.*
*But only our **diseases** did He bear*
*Himself, and our **pains** He carried.*
*And **through His bruises was***
healing granted to us.
But the Lord was pleased to crush
Him through disease."
Isaiah 53:3-5,10.

Jesus was our 'substitute' on the Cross of Calvary where He paid our debt of sin, died in our place (Jesus 'became me' at the cross), and carried our sicknesses and pains.

Other Bible translations confirm this view:-

> *"But it was **our pain** He took, and **our diseases** were put on Him..."*
> *Isaiah 53:4 (The Bible in Basic English)*

> *"However, He was the one who lifted up our **sicknesses**, and He carried our **pains**..."*
> *Isaiah 53:4 (Lexham English Bible)*

> *"Verily He suffered our **sicknesses**, and bare our **sorrows**..."*
> *Isaiah 53:4 (Wyclifffe English Bible)*

The Hebrew word for "borne" is "nasa", which means "to lift up, to bear away, to convey, or to remove to a distance" (Strongs Concordance H5375).

It is a Levitical word that applied to the scapegoat that was sent into the wilderness after the High Priest had laid his hands upon the goat (Leviticus 16:22). This action imparted the sins of Israel upon the scapegoat and sent the 'sin bearing goat' away forever into an uninhabited land.

Matthew confirms this meaning when he observes the fulfilment of Isaiah's prophecy about the Messiah, Jesus Christ:-

> *"When evening came, they brought to Him*
> *many who were demon-possessed.*
> *He drove out the spirits with a word,*
> *and healed all who were sick,*
> *So that what was spoken through the*
> *prophet Isaiah might be fulfilled:*
> ***He Himself took our weaknesses***
> ***and carried our diseases."***
> *Matthew 8:17*

> *"Sin and sickness have passed from*
> *me to Calvary – salvation and health*
> *have passed from Calvary to me."*
> *F.F. Bosworth*

6. The Testimony of Psalm 103

> *"Bless the Lord, oh my soul, and forget*
> *not all His benefits;* ***Who forgives all your***

iniquities, Who heals all your diseases."
Psalm 103:2-3

David encourages us not to forget the benefits of the Lord.

First, He *"forgives all your iniquities"*. How complete is Christ's forgiveness? We would never doubt His power to forgive us from all our sins.

> *"If we confess our sins, He is faithful and just to forgive us our sins and to cleanse us from all unrighteousness."*
> *1John 1:9*

Second, He *"heals all your diseases"*. How complete is Christ's healing? Healing is for all diseases.

That is the extent of Christ's power towards us. Just as you and I can be sure that the Lord Jesus Christ can forgive all our sins, we can be sure that the Lord Jesus Christ can heal all our sicknesses.

This wonderful Scripture reveals that the Lord's benefits are for both soul and body – *"Who forgives all"*, *"Who heals all"*.

7. The Prophecy of Malachi

"But for you who fear My name, the Sun of Righteousness shall rise with healing in His wings"
Malachi 4:2 NLT

The priest Zacharias prophesied over John the Baptist as the forerunner of The Christ Who would come as the "*dayspring from on high*" (Luke 1:78). This revealed that our Lord Jesus Christ is the "Sun of Righteousness" (Malachi 4:2) Who has risen to bring the redeeming and healing light of God to mankind.

CHAPTER THREE

DIVINE HEALING THROUGH THE SCRIPTURES

A survey of the whole Bible on divine healing clearly shows that healing has always been God's will.

Most Christian people would have no difficulty in accepting the fact that God is **able** to heal. However, many have difficulty in accepting that God is **willing** to heal them... **now**.

It is a common belief among reformers and evangelicals, for example, that "the age of miracles has passed". This is known as 'Cessationism', which is the doctrine that spiritual gifts such as speaking in tongues, prophecy, and healing ceased at the close of the 'apostolic age' in 90AD.

One of the key ideas behind this doctrine is that when the

New Testament was completed there was no further need for the availability of spiritual gifts and the miraculous in the church because the completed Bible ("*that which is perfect*") had arrived.

The 'proof text' for this doctrine is 1Corinthians 13:8-10:-

"Love never fails:
but whether there be prophecies, they shall fail;
whether there be tongues, they shall cease;
whether there be knowledge, it shall vanish away.
For we know in part, and we prophesy in part.
*But **when that which is perfect is come***
(The completed New Testament),
then that which is in part shall
***be done away** (the gifts)."*

This doctrine has given rise to much confusion concerning faith in God for divine healing and the miraculous and even the denial of the miraculous.

However, the Scriptures are clear that the miraculous works of Jesus before His ascension back into heaven were just the beginning, not the end!

> *"This **BEGINNING** of miracles did Jesus in Cana of Galilee, and manifested His glory; and His disciples believed in Him."*
> *Jn 2:11*

Luke's "Acts of the Apostles", is about the continuation of Jesus' teachings and miraculous works through the early church, which have never been rescinded or modified. This is the doctrine of 'Continuationism'.

> *"The former treatise have I made, O Theophilus, of all that Jesus **BEGAN** both to do and teach..."*
> *Acts 1:1*

A survey of the Scriptures clearly reveals that the age of healing and miracles has never stopped. In fact, every time God intervenes in human history, we see miracles. The truth of divine healing is clearly practiced throughout all Bible history and beyond.

This leaves us with the conclusion that the age of miracles has never ceased!

Divine Healing in the Wilderness

The first mention of divine healing in the scriptures is found in the Book of Exodus where the children of Israel had just been saved from their bondage in Egypt. God has intervened with miraculous power; the miraculous calling of Moses in the burning bush, the miracles and signs given to Moses and Aaron in confronting Pharaoh, the miracle of the Passover, the miracle of the Red Sea, the miracle of the bitter waters made sweet at Mara.

Here we see God giving the children of Israel an ordinance and a covenant of healing and blessing:-

> *"If you diligently heed the voice of the Lord your God and do what is right in His sight, give ear to His commandments and keep His commandments and keep His statutes I will put none of these diseases on you which I have put on Egyptians. For I am the Lord who heals you."*
> *Exodus 15:26*

The Apostle Paul declared that if the new covenant is "based on better promises" and is "more glorious", how much more shall the miracle of divine healing be evident in the church age.

> *"If the administration of the condemnation
> be glory, much more does the administration
> of righteousness exceed in glory."*
> *2 Corinthians 3:9*

Divine Healing in Israel

During the period of the kings and judges of Israel, miracles and divine healing were common, especially in the ministries of both Elijah and Elisha.

Elijah ministered divine healing to the widow's son (1 Kings 17:17-29). Elisha ministered divine healing on two occasions. The first occasion was the raising of the Shunammite's son (2Kings 5:18-37) and the second was the healing of Naaman from leprosy (2 Kings 5:1-19).

Isaiah the prophet was also used in answering the cry of King Hezekiah to be healed of sickness and extend his life (2 Kings 20 v 1-11).

These instances of divine healing show that even during the stage of Israel's apostasy, divine healing was being given by God. How much more in this age of the final outpouring of God's Spirit on the earth shall divine healing and the miracle working power of God be displayed!

Divine Healing in the Psalms

The book of Psalms has several references to the subject of divine healing. The Psalms are universally accepted as a book relevant for all ages. Many of the Psalms are prophetic, speaking of the Messiah's life and ministry.

> *"Bless the Lord, o my soul, and*
> *forget not all His benefits;*
> *Who forgives all your iniquities;*
> *Who heals all your diseases."*
> *Psalm 103:2-3*

Here we find David the inspired Psalmist declaring that God not only forgives our sins, but He also heals our diseases.

> *"He sent his Word and He healed them,*
> *and delivered them from their destructions.*
> *O that men would praise the*
> *Lord for His goodness,*
> *and for His wonderful works to*
> *the children of men!"*
> *Psalm 107:20-21*

Psalm 91 would be one of the well-known Psalms of promise to those who trust in the Lord, because it is full of promises of divine protection and blessing to those who know this secret.

The Psalm closes with the statement that whoever dwells under the shadow of the Most High will be blessed "*with long life*" and "*I will satisfy him and show him my salvation*" (Psalm 91:16).

Divine Healing in the Proverbs of Solomon

Solomon speaking words of wisdom and advice to his son, admonishes him to give attention to his words and keep them in the midst of his heart. For by doing so it will cause health to flow in his life.

> *"For they are life to those who find them, and health to all their flesh."*
> *Proverbs 4:22*

Divine Healing in the Prophets

Isaiah, who is generally regarded as the 'Messianic prophet', spoke much concerning the life and ministry of the Lord Jesus Christ and refers to healing many times in his writings. Isaiah chapter 53 would be the most notable recording that:-

> *"He is despised and left of men,*
> *a man of pains and acquainted with sickness.*
> *Surely our sicknesses He has borne, and*
> *our pains He has carried them,*
> *and we have esteemed Him plagued,*
> *smitten of God and afflicted,*
> *And He is pierced for our transgressions,*
> *bruised for our iniquities,*
> *the chastisement of our peace was upon Him,*
> *and by His bruise there is healing to us."*
> *Isaiah 53:3-5 (Dr. Young's translation)*

In proclaiming a word of judgement against the irresponsible shepherds of Israel, Ezekiel declares,

> *"The weak you have not strengthened*
> *nor have you healed those who are sick,*
> *nor bound up the broken, nor brought*
> *back what was driven away,*
> *nor sought what was lost; but with force*
> *and cruelty you have ruled them."*
> *Ezekiel 34:4*

It is very interesting to note that God expected the shepherds of Israel to minister healing to the children of Israel. But because the shepherds had drifted away from the Lord, and had lost the true purpose of their ministry, many in Israel were sick and not finding the ministry of healing from the Lord's servants.

Divine Healing in the Gospels

One of the outstanding features of the Lord Jesus Christ's ministry on earth was the power and frequency of His healing life. The Gospels are full of accounts of the healing work of the Lord Jesus Christ to suffering and sick people.

> *"The Spirit of the Lord is upon Me,*
> *because He has anointed me to*
> *preach the gospel to the poor.*
> *He has sent Me to heal the brokenhearted,*
> *to preach deliverance to the captives,*
> *and recovery of sight to the blind.*
> *To set at liberty those who are oppressed,*
> *to preach the acceptable year of the Lord."*
> *Luke 4:18-19*

The Lord Jesus Christ was constantly available to heal all who came to Him who were sick and suffering in body and in mind.

John the Baptist sent some of his disciples to Jesus to question Him, and to ask if He really was the Messiah. Jesus' reply was very clear:-

> *"Jesus answered and said to them,*
> *Go and tell John the things you*
> *have seen and heard:*
> *that the blind see, the lame walk,*
> *the lepers are cleansed,*
> *the deaf hear, the dead are raised,*
> *the poor have the gospel preached to them."*
> *Luke 7:22*

The Disciples Minister Divine Healing

When Jesus appointed the twelve Apostles He sent them to preach the gospel and to heal the sick.

> *"And when He had called His*
> *twelve disciples to Him,*
> *He gave them authority over unclean*
> *spirits, to cast them out,*
> *and to heal all kinds of sickness*
> *and all kinds of disease."*

Matt 10:1
Later Jesus appointed and sent seventy disciples to go out two by two and preach the gospel and to heal the sick.

"And heal the sick who are there and say to them, the Kingdom of God has come to you."
Luke 10:9

Divine Healing and the Great Commission

*"And He said to them,
Go into all the world and preach
the gospel to every creature.
And these signs will follow them who believe...
they will lay hands on the sick,
and they will recover.
And they went out, and preached every
where, the Lord working with them
and confirming the word through the
accompanying signs. Amen."*
Mark 16:15-20.

Prior to the Lord's ascension into heaven, He gave His final commands to the Church. This is called the 'Great Commission'. Mark and Matthew record this event with clarity.

The Lord Jesus Christ has commissioned His disciples with the task of world evangelisation. It was not a request. It was not an optional extra. It was not to be the job of a few, for in Mark He speaks of "*all who believe*". It was a command.

Divine healing the Acts of the Apostles

> *"The former treatise have I made, O Theophilus, of all that Jesus began both to do and teach."*
> *Acts 1:1*

The book of Acts is the continuation of the same healing ministry of Jesus Christ through the apostles and the early church.

> *"And fear came upon every soul; and many wonders and signs were done by the apostles"*
> *Acts 2:43*
> *"And through the hands of the apostles many signs and wonders were done among the people."*

Acts 5:12

Divine Healing in the Epistles

Paul declared that the proof of his ministry as an apostle were the miraculous healings and signs worked through him.

> *"For I lack nothing in comparison*
> *to those "super-apostles,*
> *even though I am nothing.*
> *Indeed, the signs of an apostle*
> *were performed among you*
> *with great perseverance by signs and*
> *wonders and powerful deeds."*
> *2 Corinthians 12:11-12 NET*

The apostle Paul was very conscious of the fact that signs and wonders are to accompany the preaching of the Word of God. This is because he wanted people to have faith in God and His power alone and not in their eloquence or wisdom.

> *"And my speech and my preaching*
> *was not with enticing words of man's wisdom,*

> *but in demonstration of the Spirit and of power:*
> *That your faith should not stand*
> *in the wisdom of men,*
> *but in the power of God."*
> *1Corinthians 2:4-5*

The writer of Hebrews, speaking of the apostles of the Lord, declared:-

> *"God also bearing witness, both with signs*
> *and wonders, and with different kinds of*
> *miracles, and gifts of the Holy Spirit."*
> *Hebrews 2:3-4*

Authentic Christian ministry and leadership, therefore, are characterised and identified by signs, wonders, miracles and gifts of the Holy Spirit.

The apostle of love, John, in his third epistle declares his heartfelt desire for all believers in Christ:-

> *"Beloved, I pray that you may prosper in all things*
> *and be in health, just as your soul prospers."*
> *3 John 2*

Divine Healing Declared as an Ordinance to the Church

The apostle James, a prominent leader in the early church,

outlines instructions at the close of his letter regarding the practical responses of elders, or leaders, to the situations of life.

> *"Is any among you afflicted? Let him pray.*
> *Is any merry? Let him sing psalms.*
> *Is any sick among you? Let him call*
> *for the elders of the church;*
> *and let them pray over him, anointing*
> *him with oil in the name of the Lord;*
> *and the prayer of faith shall save the sick,*
> *and the Lord shall raise him up;*
> *and if he has committed any sins,*
> *they shall be forgiven him.*
> *Confess your faults one to another,*
> *and pray one for another; that you may be healed.*
> *The effective fervent prayer of a*
> *righteous man avails much."*
> *James 5:13-16*

Divine Healing in the final book of Revelation

The ultimate experience of divine healing and health is found at the end of the age at the resurrection. Every believer's body will be resurrected and glorified to live forever in God's presence in heaven.

*"And I heard a great voice out of heaven saying,
Behold, the tabernacle of God is with
men, and He will dwell with them,
and they shall be His people, and God Himself
shall be with them, and be their God.
And God shall wipe away all tears from their eyes;
and there shall be no more death, neither sorrow,
nor crying, **neither shall there be any more pain**:
for the former things are passed away."
Rev 21:3-4*

Divine Healing in Heaven

*"And he shewed me a pure river of water of life,
clear as crystal, proceeding out of the
throne of God and of the Lamb.
In the midst of the street of it, and
on either side of the river,
was there the tree of life, which
bare twelve manner of fruits,
and yielded her fruit every month:
and the leaves of the tree were for
the **healing of the nations**.
And there shall be no more curse:
but the throne of God and of the Lamb shall be in it;*

> *and His servants shall serve Him."*
> *Rev 22:1-3*

It is abundantly clear that no command anywhere in the Scriptures has been given to change, cease or revoke God's ordinance to the Church of praying for divine healing for the sick.

All through the history of the Bible God has never ceased to show His miraculous and healing power to those suffering in their bodies.

And so today, we can believe with assurance and confidence in the unchanging healing power of our Lord Jesus Christ.

> *"Jesus Christ the same yesterday,*
> *and today, and forever."*
> *Hebrews 13:8*

CHAPTER FOUR

WHY CHRIST HEALS

A greater understanding of the reasons why the Lord Jesus Christ heals will inspire you to have greater faith and confidence in the Lord's promise to heal those who come to Him.

Here are some reasons why Christ heals.

Healing is An Expression of the Lord's Compassion

In Mark 1:40 we find the account of one of the first healings that Jesus performed in cleansing a leper. Here we read that Jesus was *"moved with compassion"* and He placed His hand on the man and healed him of his leprosy.

When the multitudes gathered and Christ fed them, the Scriptures also say that He was *"moved with compassion for them, and healed their sick" (Matthew 14:14)*.

When the blind men called out to Jesus to heal them, the Scriptures declare that Jesus "*had compassion and touched their eyes. And immediately their eyes received sight, and they followed Him*" *(Matthew 20 v 34).*

After healing the demon possessed man in the tombs who was suffering from some kind of mental illness, Jesus sent him home to his house instructing him, "*Go home to your friends, tell them what great things the Lord has done for you, and how he has had compassion on you*" *(Mark 5:19).*

When Jesus was going into the city called Nain there was a large crowd following Him. As they came near the gate of the city a funeral procession passed and a widow was weeping over her only son who was being carried to be buried.

The Scriptures declare that, *"When the Lord saw her, He had compassion on her and said to her, do not weep, then he came and touched the open coffin, and those who carried him stood still. And He said, young man, I say to you, arise. And he who was dead sat up and began to speak. And He presented him to his mother" (Luke 7:11-15).*

God's plan of redemption was an expression of his love and compassion for mankind who were lost in sin and sickness.

*"For God so loved the world that He
gave His only begotten Son,
that whoever believes in Him should not perish
but have everlasting life"*
John 3:16

*"But God demonstrates His own love towards us,
in that while we were still sinners,
Christ died for us."*
Romans 5:8

Healing is an Expression of the Goodness of God

*"God anointed Jesus of Nazareth with
the Holy Spirit and with power,
Who went about doing good and healing
all who were oppressed by the devil,
for God was with Him."*
Acts 10:38

The Scriptures abound in the declaration that divine healing is an expression of God's divine goodness. Therefore, the

Lord Jesus went about expressing that goodness of God by healing all who were sick.

Healing is an Expression of the Will of God

*"Then I said, behold, I have come –
in the volume of the book it is written of Me –
to do your will, O God."
Hebrews 10:7*

*"I can of Myself do nothing. As I hear I judge;
and My judgement is righteous,
because I do not seek My own will,
but the will of the Father who sent Me."
John 5:30*

*"For I have come down from heaven,
not to do My own will, but the
will of Him who sent Me."
John 6:38*

Because the Lord Jesus Christ was so merged with his Father. So one with His divine will and purpose. Everything that

Jesus did was the will of God. A large part of His ministry on the earth was ministering healing to the sick and suffering.

Healing is the Revealing of the Works of God

> *"Now as Jesus passed by, He saw a*
> *man who was blind from birth.*
> *And His disciples asked Him, saying Rabbi,*
> *who sinned, this man or his parents,*
> *that he was born blind?*
> *Jesus answered, neither this man*
> *nor his parents sinned,*
> *but that the works of God should*
> *be revealed in him.*
> *I must work the works of Him Who*
> *sent Me while it is day;*
> *the night is coming when no one can work."*
> *John 9:1-4*

Having said these words Jesus turned to the blind man and anointed his eyes with clay. After telling him to wash in the pool of Siloam the man was completely healed.

Healing is a work of God

After being accused of breaking the Sabbath because Jesus had healed the crippled man who was bedridden, Jesus answers the Jews with these words;

> *"The Father loves the Son, and shows*
> *Him all things that He Himself does,*
> *and He will show Him greater works*
> *than these that you may marvel."*
> *John 5:20*

When the Lord Jesus returned to his home town of Nazareth, he was rejected. The people asked the question in astonishment saying, *"Where did this man get these things? And what wisdom is this which is given to Him, that such mighty works are performed by His hands?"*

But we read they were offended at Him because they knew Him, and they held Him in contempt and wouldn't believe that He could do miracles:-

> *"Now He could do no mighty work there*
> *except that He laid His hand on a few*
> *sick people and healed them.*
> *And He marveled because of their unbelief."*
> *Mark 6:5-6*

The Lord Jesus Christ came with the express purpose of revealing the works of the Father.

Christ Healed the Sick as Proof of His Mission

> *"Do you not believe that I am in the*
> *Father and the Father in Me?*
> *The words that I speak to you, I do*
> *not speak on My own authority;*
> *but the Father who dwells in Me does the works.*
> *Believe Me that I am in the Father,*
> *and the Father in Me,*
> *or else believe Me for the sake*
> *of the works themselves."*
> *John 14:10-11*

We find that Jesus declared that his miracles proved that he was sent from God, and that because of his miracles people should listen to him.

Nicodemus, the ruler of the Jews, recognized that God was with Jesus because of the miracles and healings he performed.

*"There was a man of the Pharisees
named Nicodemus,
a ruler of the Jews.
This man came to Jesus by night and said to Him,
Rabbi, we know that You are a
teacher come from God;
for no one can do these signs that You
do, unless God is with Him."
John 3:1-2*

In His great commission to the Church Jesus commanded the disciples to go and preach the Gospel and heal the sick.

In Mark's account, the signs of miracles and healings followed as confirmation that the Lord was working with those who preached.

*"Go into the world and preach the
gospel to every person.
And these signs will follow those who believe...
they will lay hands on the sick,
and they will recover.
And they went out and preached everywhere,
the Lord working with them and confirming
the word through the accompanying signs."
Mark 15:15,17,20*

Healing is the Children's Bread

*"The woman was a Greek, a Syrophenician by birth
and she kept asking Him to cast the
demon out of her daughter.
But Jesus said to her, let the children be filled first,
for it is not good to take the children's
bread and throw it to the little dogs.
And she answered and said to Him, yes Lord,
yet even the little dogs under the table
eat from the children's crumbs."*
Mark 7:26-27

As a child of God divine healing is your inheritance. This is what Jesus meant when He said that *"healing is the children's bread"*.

Receiving healing and walking in divine health is a direct result of living at the Lord's table. In our natural families, our children take it for granted that they will be fed food daily. This is their right, their inheritance as being part of the family and the responsibility of parents to provide for them.

In speaking to this woman Jesus was declaring that Divine healing is the inheritance of every child of God. But because of her faith, as a heathen woman, she pressed through and received healing.

How much more shall you as a child of God receive healing in your body.

Healing Brings Glory to God

There is no doubt that the hearts of people rejoice and give glory to God when a miracle of healing is seen by their own eyes.

> *"Then great multitudes came to Him*
> *having with them those who were lame,*
> *blind, mute, maimed and many others;*
> *and they laid them down at Jesus'*
> *feet, and He healed them.*
> *So that multitude marveled when*
> *they saw the mute speaking,*
> *the maimed made whole, the lame*
> *walking, and the blind seeing;*
> *and they glorified the God of Israel."*
> *Matthew 15:30*

Jesus declared the intention of His raising of Lazarus from the dead:-

> *"When Jesus heard that, He said, this*

> *sickness is not unto death,
> but for the glory of God, that the Son of
> God may be glorified through it."*
> *John 11:4*

The same result was effected in the heart's of the people who were looking on when Jesus healed the paralytic and forgave him his sins.

> *"He said to the paralytic, arise, take up
> your bed, and go to your house.
> And he arose and departed to his house.
> Now when the multitude saw it, they
> marveled and glorified God,
> who had given such power to men."*

Christ Heals to Fulfill the Prophecy of Scripture

One of the universally accepted prophecies predicting the healing ministry of the Messiah is found in Isaiah 53:4.

> *"Surely He has borne our griefs (pains)
> and carried our sorrows (sicknesses)."*

The Apostle Matthew writing under the inspiration of the Holy Spirit declared that Christ's ministry was a direct fulfillment of this prophecy of Isaiah.

> *"When the evening was come,*
> *they brought unto Him many that*
> *were possessed with devils;*
> *and He cast out the spirits with His*
> *word, and healed all that were sick,*
> *that it might be fulfilled that was*
> *spoken by Isaiah the prophet,*
> *saying, Himself took our infirmities*
> *and bare our sicknesses."*
> *Matthew 8:16-17*

Here we see the principle of the Scripture interpreting Scripture.

There is no need for any further explanation or interpretation. We can clearly see that the Lord Jesus Christ atoned for our sicknesses and diseases on the cross.

Finally, the apostle Peter also interprets Isaiah's prophecy when he wrote under the inspiration of the Holy Spirit:-

*"Who Himself bore our sins in
His own body on the tree,
that we, having died to sins, should
live unto righteousness:
by Whose stripes you were healed."
1Peter 2:24*

CHAPTER FIVE

DIVINE HEALING IN YOUR FAITH

*"A certain woman, who had an issue
of blood for twelve years,
and had suffered many things by many physicians,
and had spent all that she had, and was
no better, but rather grew worse,
having heard the things concerning Jesus,
came up behind Him in the crowd,
and touched His clothes.
For she said, "If I just touch His
clothes, I will be made well."
Immediately the flow of her blood was dried up,
and she felt in her body that she
was healed of her affliction.
Immediately Jesus, perceiving in Himself
that the power had gone out from Him,
turned around in the crowd, and asked,
"Who touched My clothes?"
His disciples said to Him, "You see the
multitude pressing against You,*

and You say, 'Who touched Me?'"
He looked around to see her
who had done this thing.
But the woman, fearing and trembling,
knowing what had been done to her,
came and fell down before Him,
and told Him all the truth.
He said to her, "Daughter, your faith
has made you whole (well).
Go in peace, and be cured of your disease."
Mk 5:25-34; Lk 8:43-4

This is an account of a woman's faith. What she did and her subsequent healing shows us what we can do to release our faith for a miracle.

Activating our faith

A few years ago my children gave me a GPS computer for my cycling and because I was so busy with work and other commitments, I left it in my office and continued using the old manual speedo. Finally, months later, I replaced the old one and activated the GPS and a whole new world opened up for me...time, speed, heart rate, calorie burning.

Nothing happened in this 'new dimension' of GPS for me, until I got active and switched on my device that it all worked!

In other words, I had to switch on my GPS to start receiving the data!

It's the same concept with our faith for a miracle. We need to 'switch on our faith' in order to receive our miracle!

> *Miracles don't just happen,*
> *we need to 'work our miracle'*
> *through activating our faith*

It is important to notice that the apostle Paul identified the gift for miracles as the gift of *"working of miracles"* (1Cor 12:10).

This is true for every gift given to us by God. We must activate them through faith. That's the way everything works in God.

> *"But **without faith it is impossible to please Him**:*
> *for he that comes to God **must believe** that He is,*
> *and that He is a **rewarder** of them that*
> ***diligently seek Him**." Heb 11:6*

FAITH IS NOT PASSIVE, FAITH IS ALWAYS ACTIVE

A picture of this kind of 'passive faith' is seen at the Pool of Bethesda where so many people were waiting for the waters to move, external to their own faith, and so, were not healed.

> *"In these lay a great multitude of impotent folk, of blind, halt, withered,* ***waiting for the moving of the water.****"*
> *Jn 5:3*

When we wait for something to happen, we delay our miracle. Activating our faith in the 'now', or present, is how we begin to 'work our miracle'.

In this account of the woman's healing, in Mark chapter five, we learn about a person who demonstrated 'activated faith'.

There are eight things that she did and experienced that released her miracle.

The first thing that she did was to come to a **decision**. She came to an end of her own efforts, energy and ideas and aligned her faith in God.

> *"And a certain woman which had an issue of blood **twelve years...** And had **suffered many things of many physicians**, and had **spent all** that she had, and was nothing bettered, but rather **grew worse**."*

This poor woman was so desperate. She had tried everything, spent everything, engaged the help and treatment of everyone available to her, but she was still suffering pain from her condition, in fact, she was getting worse.

One day she decided that she had had enough. She was so desperate for a change in her circumstances and her words and actions showed it. She decided she was going to get healed!

Second, she **heard the message of healing in Jesus Christ and believed it**.

> *"When she had heard of Jesus..."*
> *Something changed inside of her when she heard the message of healing in Jesus Christ and her faith clicked into gear. Her faith made her confident and she knew that her miracle was at hand.*

The context of the story was that she decided in her faith that she was healed long before she was healed in her body by Jesus. This is so important to understand in order to operate faith for our miracle! Her faith was engaged before she was physically healed.

She decided 'in her faith' that she was healed long before she was healed in her body.

Just like this woman, we must confidently know that it is God's will to heal us and make us a whole person. Just like the forgiveness of our sins, healing is an exchange that Jesus Christ secured for us and actioned for us in His atoning work in our place on the cross.

> *"Who His own self bare our sins in*
> *His own body on the tree,*
> *that we, being dead to sins, should*
> *live unto righteousness:*
> *by Whose stripes you were healed."*
> 1Pet 2:24

Sin and sickness have passed from me to Calvary,
Salvation and health have passed
from Calvary to me!
F.F. Bosworth

Third, she created a '**faith image**' on the the inside of her of Jesus healing her. She began to think of being healed and she began to talk to herself about being healed long before she even met Jesus!

Her faith was so strong that she **saw herself being healed by Jesus** and planned to get to Him and touch His clothes.

She found herself constantly thinking and confessing healing to herself, in her heart and mind, even though she wasn't physically healed yet! She had **decided in her faith** that she was healed. The physical healing would follow later!

> *"For she said, If I may touch but*
> *His clothes, I shall be whole"*
> *Mk 5:28*

> *"For **she kept saying (within herself)**,*
> *If I only touch His garments, I shall*
> *be restored to health."*
> *AMPLIFIED BIBLE*

> *"...because she **thought**..."*
> *NIV*

This is such an important key to releasing our healing; we receive our healing in our faith first, before we receive healing in our bodies!

**We get healed in our FAITH first,
Then give healing to our BODIES**

She came to a revelation and decision in her faith about her healing long before she was physically healed.

Fourth, she was **very specific about her healing.** She knew her need and went after the answer from Jesus for her healing.

*"...she declared to Him in the
presence of all the people
THE REASON she had touched Him..."*

*"Now faith is the substance of **THINGS** hoped for,
the evidence of **THINGS** not seen."
Heb 11:1*

What is the '**THING**' that you need from God today? Be like this woman and decide in your faith that your miracle is on its way!

> *"Therefore I tell you, all the **THINGS**
> you pray and ask for
> **BELIEVE that you HAVE received them**,
> and you **WILL HAVE** them."*
> *Mk 11:24 - HCSB*

> *"But seek first the kingdom of
> God, and His righteousness;
> and all these **THINGS** shall be added unto you."*
> *Matt 6:33*

Fifth, she used a **'POINT OF CONTACT'** TO **RELEASE HER FAITH**.

The great evangelist, Oral Roberts, was a modern day pioneer of the concept and use of a 'point of contact' when he encouraged people who were sick to reach out and touch their TV screen as their 'point of contact' to release healing. Many people were healed doing this.

It is important to notice that this woman decided to make the border of Jesus' garment her 'point of contact' for the release of her miracle. We have discovered that God will honour any point of contact that will help us release our faith.

There are three important things to understand about a 'point of contact':-

A POINT OF CONTACT is given as a MEANS of helping us to RELEASE OUR FAITH. It is important to understand that a point of contact isn't 'magic', or supernatural…it's a MEANS TO RELEASE FAITH!

A POINT OF CONTACT is something TANGIBLE AND PRACTICAL, it is something we 'DO in faith', and when we DO IT we RELEASE OUR FAITH TOWARD GOD.

A POINT OF CONTACT SETS THE TIME for the release of our faith for our miracle. Our miracle begins at the point of faith, not at the point of physical healing.

> *"For she said, **"If I can just touch His robes, I'll be made well!"** **Instantly** her flow of blood ceased, and she sensed in her body that she was cured of her affliction."*

Mk 5:28-29

Some other examples of 'points of contact' in the Scriptures are:-

- Naaman **dipped 7 times** in the river Jordan for healing

- The widow **gave her last meal** to Elijah for provision

- The women **built a room** for Elisha for the healing of her son

- The blind man **washed** his eyes to see

- The ten leper's went to **show the priest** they were healed

- **Handkerchiefs and aprons** were prayed over by Paul and laid on the sick

- James instructs the pastors to **anoint with oil** and **lay on hands** for healing

- The Macedonians **sowed seeds of finance** to produce a harvest of financial provision

- Paul instructed us to **confess our faith** for salvation

Many churches today offer '**altar calls**' in services for healing

> *"Her confession of faith*
> *cleared a way for her feet*
> *to get through the crowd*
> *and made an opening*
> *to get to Jesus."*
> **Oral Roberts**

NOTHING WAS GOING TO PREVENT HER FROM GETTING TO JESUS AND RECEIVING HER MIRACLE!

Six, **she made contact with the healing power of Christ.**

> *"And straight away the fountain*
> *of her blood was dried up;*
> *and she **felt in her body** that she*
> *was healed of that plague.*
> *And Jesus, immediately knowing in Himself*
> *that **VIRTUE (power)** had gone out of Him..."*
> Mk 5:30 KJV

Contact was made between her faith and the healing power resident in the Lord Jesus Christ...DIVINE HEALING! Christ's healing power is still available today and it is through our faith that contact is made.

> *"And when He had called unto
> Him His twelve disciples,
> He gave them power against unclean
> spirits, to cast them out,
> and to heal all manner of sickness
> and all manner of diseases."*
> *Matt 10:1*

Seven, **the faith that she released made her whole.** It is important to notice that Jesus' clothes didn't heal her, or her confession, or even her decision to be healed. it was her **activated faith**, the faith that she released to Jesus Christ and His divine power that healed her.

> *"And He said to her, Daughter,*
> ***YOUR FAITH*** *has made you* ***WHOLE..."***

FAITH IS ALWAYS IN THE NOW

> *"**NOW** faith **IS**...
> ...the **substance** of things hoped for,
> the **evidence** of **things not seen**."*
> *Heb 11:1*

Faith is not about what we have, What we can see, or what we already possess,

FAITH IS ABOUT THE THINGS NOT SEEN!

> *"Therefore I tell you, all the things*
> *you pray and ask for*
> ***BELIEVE*** *that you* ***HAVE*** *received them,*
> *and you* ***WILL HAVE*** *them."*
> *Mk 11:24 - HCSB*

Eight, Jesus made her **WHOLE.**

> *"And He said to her, Daughter,*
> *your faith has made you* ***WHOLE****;*
> *go* ***IN PEACE****, and be* ***WHOLE*** *of your plague."*
> *Mk 5:34*

This woman received much more than she hoped for. She desperately wanted physical healing, but Jesus gave her what her whole inner being had been crying out for; **PEACE.**

Jesus made an important connection between healing and peace, because in God's view, the atoning provision of

Jesus Christ is **WHOLENESS,** that is, the **TOTAL HEALING OF THE SOUL, MIND AND BODY!**

And so, we discover that healing from God is both spiritual and physical.

> *"Who His own Self bare our **sins** in*
> *His own body on the tree,*
> *that we, being dead to sins, should*
> *live unto righteousness:*
> *by Whose stripes you were **healed**."*
> *1Pet 2:24*

> *"And the very God of peace sanctify you **wholly**;*
> *and I pray God your **whole spirit***
> ***and soul and body***
> *be preserved blameless*
> *unto the coming of our Lord Jesus Christ."*
> *1Thess 5:23*

This woman came to Jesus for **healing in her body** and also received **healing in her soul.**

She discovered God's priority:-

GOD'S PRIORITY IS THE HEALING OF MY

SOUL

CHAPTER SIX

HEALING AND THE MINISTRY OF LAYING ON OF HANDS

*"And **these signs shall follow them that believe**;*
In my name they shall cast out devils;
they shall speak with new tongues;
They shall take up serpents;
and if they drink any deadly thing,
it shall not hurt them;
they shall lay hands on the sick,
and they shall recover.*"*
Mark 16:17- 18

The Bible is full of examples of the practice of "the laying on of hands" by a minister of God for the activation of faith and the impartation of divine healing.

The Lord Jesus Christ regularly used this practice when ministering healing to the sick.

> *"When the sun was setting,*
> *all those who had any that were sick with*
> *various diseases brought them to Him;*
> *and He laid His hands on every one*
> *of them, and healed them."*
> *Luke 4:40*

He also included the practice of laying on of hands in the commissioning instructions to His disciples when He sent them to evangelise the world.

> *"Go into all the world, and preach*
> *the gospel to every creature...*
> *they will lay hands on the sick,*
> *and they will recover."*
> *Mark 16:16-18*

The apostle James included the ministry of healing, through the laying on of hands with the "anointing with oil", as a role and responsibility of the elders, or leaders, of the church.

> *"Is any sick among you? let him call*

*for the elders of the church;
and let them pray over him, anointing
him with oil in the name of the Lord:
And the prayer of faith shall save the
sick, and the Lord shall raise him up;
and if he have committed sins,
they shall be forgiven him."*
James 5:14-15

This outward action of reaching out physically to the sick and the hurting demonstrates an inner exercise of faith and compassion by the minister of God. The oil and the laying on of hands becomes the 'point of contact' to release faith and impart healing power.

This inner faith comes from a heart full of expectation and confidence that divine healing will flow through the prayer of faith.

We have discovered that creating an atmosphere that promotes and encourages faith for healing is very important, especially in church services. We can do this in the following ways.

First, music is one of the most important ways to create a positive atmosphere for faith. Choosing songs that speak of God's power and ability to do the impossible is very important and the use of background music while in prayer all help to create an atmosphere where faith is encouraged and activated.

Second, the reading of Scriptures about divine healing is important because "*faith comes by hearing the Word of God*" (Rom 10:17).

Third, testimonies and stories of healing bring proof of the reality of divine healing for today, especially if the person sharing their story of divine healing is known by the hearers.

Fourth, the exercise of the gift of "*the word of knowledge*" (1Cor 12:8) can greatly increase people's faith for healing, especially if the person exercising this gift does not know the people needing healing.

The more specific and precise the "*word of knowledge*", the more helpful and impacting it can be. For example, specific descriptions of the condition, pain or disease, location of pain, length of sickness, age and description of the sufferer. All of these details create an atmosphere for faith because the knowledge shared has been received by revelation and not observation.

William Branham, a healing pioneer, frequently used specific words of knowledge in describing people he would pray for. For example, names, sex, age, exact description of the sickness or condition. All of this created such an atmosphere of faith for healing.

Fifth, great preaching and teaching on the message of faith, the miraculous and divine healing will stir people's hearts, bring clarity and understanding that divine healing is available to them and encourage the sick and hurting to reach out in faith to their loving and healing God.

How to operate the Laying on of hands

It is important to move slowly and gently, while explaining to people what we are doing. We must never mistake power for noise, or human energy.

The secret is to be able to tap into the power of the Holy Spirit and impart Divine healing through faith.

And so, when ministering the laying on of hands place a hand very gently on a persons upper forehead, praying the prayer of faith and pronouncing divine healing and health over them in the Name of Jesus.

> *"...in My Name...they shall lay hands on the sick, and they shall recover."*
> *Mk 16:18*

CHAPTER SEVEN

BELIEVING IN THE WAIT

What do we do when our healing or miracle doesn't happen straight away when we pray and we find ourselves 'in the wait'?

When we find ourselves 'in the wait' has God left us? Does this mean that we don't have faith or it's not God's will to heal us? Is God against us or have we done something wrong?

We have discovered that none of these common questions adequately answer the why of 'the wait', which we all have experienced and will experience at some point.

The Scriptures teach us that staying in faith, no matter what the situation, is the important thing for every 'believer'. This is known as 'faithfulness' in the Bible because faithfulness is faith in the long run.

Sometimes God will take us the long way to get us where He wants us to be

Our faith will help us realise that God always loves us and His intentions and plans towards us are always good! We can always be confident of that fact!

> *"Surely goodness and loving kindness*
> *shall follow me all the days of my life,*
> *and I will dwell in the house of the Lord forever."*
> *Ps 23:6*

Examples of 'the Wait'

Our "father of faith", Abraham, experienced a very long delay between the promise given to him by God and the provision of his and Sarah's miracle son Isaac...for 25 years!

Yet Abraham was never condemned by God for lacking faith because he had to wait for the miracle. On the contrary, he is applauded as our "Father of faith" (Rom 4:16).

Another example of 'the wait' in the Scriptures is the account of Daniel's prayer. After he prayed, a 21 day delay occurred because of the massive spiritual warfare needed to answer his prayers.

*"Then he said to me, Don't be afraid, Daniel;
for from the first day that you set
your heart to understand,
and to humble yourself before your
God, your words were heard:
and I have come for your words' sake.
But the prince of the kingdom of Persia
withstood me twenty-one days;
but, behold, Michael, one of the
chief princes, came to help me:
for I had been left alone with the kings of Persia."
Dan 10:13-14*

It is important to understand that there are often significant spiritual ramifications that start occurring the moment we pray and believe for a miracle.

The key is to find a place of faith where our trust is in our Lord Jesus alone and not in what is or what is not happening around us.

Faith is more than a transactional thing we do to get something from God. Instead, faith is a relational connection with God that has nothing to do with our circumstances.

Faith is a relationship connection with God

Faith is the mode of our spirit that causes us to constantly look to God and trust Him in every situation and at every time; whether good or bad, easy or difficult. This kind of indomitable faith empowers us and strengthens us through every circumstance of life.

> *"I know both how to be abased,*
> *and I know how to abound:*
> *every where and in all things I am instructed*
> *both to be full and to be hungry,*
> *both to abound and to suffer need.*
> *I can do all things through Christ*
> *who strengthens me."*
> *Phil 4:13-14*

We must not get 'the cart in front of the donkey'. In other words, our faith leads us into our miracle, not our miracle leads us into faith.

This view of faith can cause us to think that if we don't receive a miracle, or have to wait, we mustn't have faith. But this couldn't be further from the truth. Our faith always comes first because our trust is in God, not a miracle.

We don't have faith because we have received a miracle, We receive a miracle because we have faith!

Here's the thing about healing miracles: We can't heal ourselves.

Only the Lord Jesus Christ has the power to heal miraculously.

Therefore, it is futile to strive and struggle to 'get more faith' for a miracle. This approach only heightens our anxiety, rather than our faith and trust in God.

Mustard-Seed Sized Faith

So how much faith do we need for a miracle?

Jesus said that if we have *"faith the size of a mustard seed"* (Matt 17:20), nothing would be impossible for us…and that's a very small measure indeed.

Our part in any miracle is the 'small part', or the 'faith part'. God never expects us to do the miracle because that's His part, the 'big part'.

God has chosen the way of faith to release His awesome, miracle power, because, "without faith it is impossible to please God" (Heb 11:6).

**NEVER COMPARE THE SIZE OF THE MOUNTAIN,
TO THE SIZE OF YOUR FAITH,
ALWAYS COMPARE THE SIZE OF THE MOUNTAIN
TO THE SIZE OF YOUR GOD!**

Another common danger can be to view divine healing as 'faith healing', or, to have 'faith in my faith', rather than divine healing, which is faith in God, our Divine healer.

It is God who works the miracle, hence, divine healing.

Not all miracles are instant

So, is it realistic to expect that every healing and miracle will be instant, every time we pray?

The Scriptures, and our experience, indicate that healings and miracles are not all instant, or an everyday occurrence, otherwise, miracles would be normal and no longer miraculous. This is why they are called miracles, because they are, "a marvelous event manifesting a supernatural act" (Concise English Dictionary).

To project and expect a life filled with every day, instant and constant miracles every time we pray is just simply unrealistic and will eventually lead us to disappointment.

We are called to live our life of faith in an imperfect, limited, physical world where our connection with the Holy Spirit is "in part", or "fragmentary";

> *"For our knowledge is fragmentary*
> *(incomplete and imperfect),*
> *and our prophecy (our teaching) is*
> *fragmentary (incomplete and imperfect)."*
> *1Cor 13:9 AMPLIFIED BIBLE*

So how should we live then in this imperfect world? With unwavering faith and confidence in God.

With a faith in God that trusts Him no matter what the circumstance or outcome.

Understanding how God works

Sometimes we are delivered '**IN**' the circumstance (or

'Instantly'), sometimes we are delivered '**THROUGH**' the circumstance (or 'progressively') and ultimately we will be delivered '**OUT**' of the circumstance (or 'permanently') when we die.

The choice is God's alone to make about how we receive a miracle...after all He knows everything about everyone and is kind, loving and just, seeking our highest good.

My experience also shows me that sometimes we can be experiencing God delivering us '**IN**' ('instantly') a situation and delivering us '**THROUGH**' ('progressively') another situation at the same time.

However, God doesn't always work instantly, even though we all love those instant miracles, those moments when God removes our problem right now!

God can use our choices, our willingness to change our attitude, lifestyle and habits and seeking the best medical advice and treatments in order to lead us into health and strength progressively.

Ultimately, God will deliver us all '**OUT**' ('permanently') of this life through death, or at the second coming of the Lord Jesus Christ..."*and so shall we be ever with the Lord.*" (1Thess 4:17)

As humans we resist this idea because we so want to hold onto this life. But God has ordained that death is not the end. It is the doorway of deliverance and transference from an imperfect, limited, physical life into a perfect, eternal, spiritual life with Christ.

> *"For we know that if our earthly house*
> *of this tabernacle were dissolved,*
> *we have a building of God, an house not*
> *made with hands, eternal in the heavens.*
> *For in this we groan,*
> *earnestly desiring to be clothed upon with*
> *our house which is from heaven...*
> *We are confident, I say, and willing rather to be*
> *absent from the body, and to be*
> *present with the Lord."*
> *2Cor 5:1-2, 8*

> *"And God shall wipe away all tears from their eyes;*
> *and there shall be no more death,*
> *neither sorrow, nor crying,*
> *neither shall there be any more pain:*
> *for the former things are passed away."*
> *Rev 21:4*

Our calling, therefore, is to trust and obey God and His Word 'IN', 'THROUGH' and 'OUT' of every situation as God chooses. The moment we place an instant requirement on God, we are placing a limit on how God can work in our lives and circumstances. The further we walk with God, we begin to understand and appreciate His varied and marvellous workings.

The will of God always makes sense looking back

Why does the will of God always look unclear looking forward? Because God works through faith. He requires us to obey and act on His Word when there is no evidence.

> **'The wait' causes us to believe with no physical evidence... our faith is our evidence.**

"Now faith is...the evidence of things not seen."
Heb 11:1

When we look back on our life we can often see the hand of God in our lives and the reasons why His timing is perfect!

Never stop praying and believing

If Jesus needed to pray twice for a blind man to be healed, maybe we need to be more persistent in our faith.

"He came to Bethsaida.
They brought a blind man to Him,
and begged Him to touch him.
He took hold of the blind man by the hand,
and brought him out of the village.
When He had spit on his eyes,
and laid His hands on him,
He asked him if he saw anything.
He looked up, and said, "I see men;
for I see them like trees walking."
Then again He laid His hands on his eyes.
He looked intently, and was restored,
and saw everyone clearly. "
Matt 8:22-25

Also, we see how the 10 lepers were healed by Jesus *"as they went"* to the temple. Jesus asked them to go to the priest without any evidence of being healed. But "*as they went*" they were healed. Often, our healing occurs as we obey God.

> *"As He entered into a certain village,*
> *ten men who were lepers met Him,*
> *who stood at a distance.*
> *They lifted up their voices, saying,*
> *"Jesus, Master, have mercy on us!"*
> *When He saw them, He said to them, "Go*
> *and show yourselves to the priests."*
> *It happened that as they went,*
> *they were cleansed. "*
> *Lk 17:12-14*

When we find ourselves 'in the wait' for our miracle, we are among great company. We are experiencing the same things as the illustrious company of saints who have gone before us; who "*died in faith not having received the promise*".

> *"And these all, having obtained a*
> *good report through faith,*
> *received not the promise."*
> *Heb 11:39*

Never stop doing the possible

When we find ourselves 'in the wait', we should never stop believing and 'doing the possible', that is, praying, reading the Word of God, being in church, serving others, eating right, exercising, resting and rejuvenating, visiting our doctor and keeping a positive, faith attitude.

When we keep doing these things consistently that are possible, we will find ourselves constantly positioned for God to do the impossible and work our miracle in His time and in His way.

DO THE POSSIBLE
AND BELIEVE GOD FOR THE IMPOSSIBLE

This is faith demonstrated 'in the wait'. It is the kind of faith that recognises that God is always working...but not necessarily in the time, or in the way that we want Him to.

GOD IS ALWAYS WORKING,
BUT NOT NECESSARILY IN THE WAY,
OR IN THE TIME THAT WE WANT HIM TO!

Always pray and do not faint

"And He spoke a parable to them to this end,
that men ought always to pray, and not to faint;
*Saying, There was in a city a judge, who
feared not God, neither regarded man:
And there was a widow in that city;
and she came unto him, saying,
Avenge me of mine adversary. And
he would not for a while:
but afterward he said within himself,
Though I fear not God, nor regard man;
Yet because this widow troubles
me, I will avenge her,
lest by her continual coming she weary me."
Lk 18:1-5*

CONCLUSION

GOD'S PRIORITY IS THE HEALING OF YOUR SOUL

God's priority is the healing of our soul; our mind, emotions, heart and inner being.

When our soul is healthy our life is healthy! That's why God makes the healing of our souls His priority.

A restored soul equals a restored life.

When we are healthy on the inside it effects every area of our lives.

> *"A sound heart is the life of the flesh."*
> *Prov 14:30*

> *"Guard your heart with all diligence;*
> *for out of it are the issues of life."*

Prov 4:23 (NET Bible)
King David discovered this truth and wrote:-

> *"The Lord is my shepherd*
> *I shall not want...*
> *...**HE RESTORES MY SOUL...**"*
> *Ps 23:1,3*

...and...

> *"Behold, the eye of the LORD is*
> *upon them that fear him,*
> *upon them that hope in his mercy;*
> *To **deliver their soul from death**,*
> *and to keep them alive in famine."*
> *Ps 33:18-19*

The apostle John also understood this truth when he wrote that physical prosperity and health flow from a soul that is "prospering" on the inside. The International Standard Version translates this way; *"just as your soul is healthy"*.

> *"Beloved, I wish above all things*
> *that you may **prosper** and be in **health**,*
> *even as your **soul prospers**."*
> *3Jn 2*

The apostle Paul also understood this truth when he prayed

that the Thessalonians would be "*sanctified completely and preserved blameless*" for Christ, in their "*whole spirit, soul and body.*"

> *"And the very God of peace sanctify you wholly; and I pray God your whole spirit and soul and body be preserved blameless unto the coming of our Lord Jesus Christ."*
> *1Thess 5:23*

However, along the way of life our inner person, or soul, can become damaged by the effects of sin and living a life away from God.

The Scriptures variously describe this 'inner damage' as:-

> **"A wounded spirit"**
> *"The spirit of a man will sustain his infirmity; but a **wounded spirit** who can bear?"*
> *Prov 18:14*

> **"A broken spirit"**
> *"A merry heart makes a cheerful countenance: but by sorrow of the heart the **spirit is broken**."*
> *Prov 15:13*

*"**A defiled spirit**"*
*"Therefore, since we have these promises,
dear friends, let us cleanse ourselves
from everything that could **defile
the body and the spirit**,
and thus accomplish holiness out
of reverence for God."
2Cor 7:1*

*"**A bitter heart**"*
*"The **heart knows its own bitterness**,
and with its joy no one else can share."
Prov 14:10*

Christ is our Wholeness

God's purpose in His provision of Christ is our wholeness, that is, the healing of our total self - spirit, soul, mind and body.

So how are we healed in our souls, or hearts?

The Bible teaches us that we are healed in our soul, or heart, when the power of the Lord Jesus Christ forgives, cleanses and heals us from our sin and our old life and makes us "*new creations*" on the inside.

> *"Therefore, if anyone is in Christ,*
> *he is a new creation:*
> *old things have passed away; behold,*
> *all things have become new."*
> *2Cor 5:17*

> *"Not by works of righteousness*
> *which we have done,*
> *but according to His mercy He saved us,*
> *by the washing of regeneration, and*
> *renewing of the Holy Spirit."*
> *Titus 3:5*

The Bible teaches that to be healed in our souls we must personally do these things:-

1. **ACKNOWLEDGE** my sin

2. **BELIEVE** that the Lord Jesus Christ is the only answer for the forgiveness of my sin

3. **REPENT** and turn from my sin

4. **RECEIVE** Jesus Christ as my personal Saviour and Lord

5. **COMMIT** to a life of following, pleasing and serving the Lord Jesus Christ

Your Personal Invitation to Receive Christ

*"But as many as received Him,
to them He gave the power to
become children of God."
John 1:12*

To receive Jesus Christ means to open the door of your life and invite Jesus to come in as Saviour and Lord.

If you would like to accept this invitation, pray this prayer now.

PRAYER OF SALVATION

*"Dear Lord Jesus,
I know that I am a sinner and I come to you for forgiveness.
I believe that you died for my sin.
I now repent from my sin.
I invite you, Jesus Christ, to come into
my life as Saviour and Lord.
Wash me and make me clean on the inside.
Make me a new person.
I am willing to follow You and serve*

GOD'S PRIORITY IS THE HEALING OF YOUR SOUL

*You all the days of my life.
Amen."*

If you prayed this prayer of salvation it's very important to understand these two things.

First, you can be totally assured that the Lord Jesus Christ will answer your prayer of faith. You will not be disappointed.

You will begin to feel different on the inside as the Holy Spirit begins His work of bringing forgiveness, cleansing and healing in your heart.

*"If you will confess with your
mouth that Jesus is Lord,
and believe in your heart that God raised
Him from the dead, you will be saved.
For with the heart, one believes
unto righteousness;
and with the mouth confession
is made unto salvation.
For the Scripture says, "Whoever believes
in Him will not be disappointed."
Rom 10:9-10*

Second, it is so important to follow up your decision today

by connecting with a Bible believing, spirit empowered church that will be able to help you to live your new found faith in Jesus Christ.

> *"And the Lord added to the church daily*
> *those who were being saved."*
> *Acts 2:42*

If you don't know of a good church look online at the following website of my church and someone will help you get connected, wherever you are...www.c3bd.com

GUIDELINES FOR CHRISTIAN LIVING

1. Daily Bible Readings

The Bible is God's message to you. In it you will find out how to live the Christian life.

Obey God's word and your life will be contented, satisfying and powerful.

2. Daily Prayer

When you pray, God is present and hears you. Talk to Him every day and set aside a time each day for prayer.

3. Open Confession Of Christ

Start today and tell someone what you have done in receiving Christ. Talk to a pastor about sealing your decision through water Baptism (Acts 2:38).

4. Fellowship With Christians In Church Life

Make friends with eager Christians. Through fellowship with others in church services and small groups you will grow in Christian knowledge, experience and confidence. The New Testament teaches that every Christian is a member of a local church.

5. Serve Christ

You are saved to serve. Seek an area of service in your local church immediately. Be ready to study and learn and to develop your gifts and abilities for Christ's service.

BIBLIOGRAPHY

"Christ the Healer", F.F. Bosworth

"If you need healing do these things", Oral Roberts

"How you can be healed", Gordon Lindsay

"The new John G. Lake Sermons", Gordon Lindsay

"Answers and Questions Concerning Divine Healing", Gordon Lindsay

"The Healing Word", David Foot

"When evening came, they brought to Him many who were demon-possessed. He drove out the spirits with a word and HEALED all who were sick, so that what was spoken through the prophet Isaiah might be FULFILLED: "He Himself took our weaknesses and CARRIED OUR DISEASES."
Matthew 8:16-17

DR GORDON MOORE
BOOKS

EMAIL RECEPTION@C3BD.COM TO ORDER

GOING TO THE NEXT LEVEL

GORDON MOORE

LEADERSHIP STYLES & LEVELS OF CHURCH

GORDON MOORE

Yes HOLY SPIRIT

GORDON MOORE

ASCENT

GORDON MOORE
A DEVOTIONAL JOURNAL OF FAITH

BLENDER families

GORDON MOORE

STORY

GORDON MOORE

TAKE SOMEONE WITH YOU

GORDON MOORE

www.ingramcontent.com/pod-product-compliance
Lightning Source LLC
LaVergne TN
LVHW052255070426
835507LV00035B/2937